Dauntless

Dauschlann

Dumitdiana

Daughters

Dorothea

Dandelion

Desenchères

Dauntless

Dandelion

Dandelion

Demolition

Dauntless

Dauntless

Dandelion

Dandelion

Dumortiera

Made in the USA
Monee, IL
26 December 2023